# TURNER, BOLTON, AND WEBB

*Three Historians of the American Frontier*

Wilbur R. Jacobs, John W. Caughey,
and Joe B. Frantz

# TURNER, BOLTON, and WEBB

## Three Historians of the American Frontier

UNIVERSITY OF WASHINGTON PRESS
Seattle and London

Lectures originally delivered at the 1963 meeting of the
Western History Association, these essays appeared in a condensed form in the Winter, 1964, issue of *The American West*.

# FOREWORD

Looming large in American historiography are three historians, Frederick Jackson Turner, Herbert Eugene Bolton, and Walter Prescott Webb, who are here grouped together as historians of the West.

Curiously, Turner, whose theories initiated a new approach to the study of the American West, never considered himself a western historian and resented such a narrow definition of his field. Bolton, who trained more specialists on the West than any other man, is generally thought of as a Latin Americanist, though the bulk of his own work fits within the boundaries of the United States. Webb, whose field of interest seemed to be firmly within the traditional confines of the romantic West, ended by generalizing on the whole world.

The three, furthermore, did not conceive of the West—and its concomitant feature, the frontier—in the same definition of time, place, and significance.

For Turner, the frontier was part of an historical process exemplified by the late colonial and early national West east of the Mississippi. For Bolton, the frontier was everywhere in the Americas, provided the historian took off his blinders, began looking in 1492 instead of 1763, and taught himself that a frontier could be French, or Dutch, or Portuguese, or Spanish as well as English. For Bolton, as he is seen in his translations and biographies, the West might better have been called the North. His favorite frontier was the one that the Spaniards pushed north from the islands and Mexico into Florida and New Mexico, Texas and Pimería, Louisiana and California. For Webb, the West centered in the arid plains of the Trans-Mississippi

West, though eventually his frontier was to encompass the whole of three continents which the Europeans explored and exploited in the age of discovery.

In addition to training many young scholars, these three historians profoundly influenced innumerable others. Both Turner and Bolton saw schools of history rise around them. Bolton was a prolific writer, and Webb, though more sporadic as a producer, reached a wide audience. Yet Turner, the sparsity of whose writings distressed his regents at Wisconsin, had by far the greatest influence on historical thought in the nation.

All three demonstrated a capacity to make what might be called journeyman contributions to the historical record: Turner in his monograph on *Rise of the New West,* Bolton in many detailed studies of the advances into the Spanish Borderlands, and Webb in *The Texas Rangers, The Handbook of Texas, Flat Top,* and various other titles. Their identifying contributions, however, lie in their bolder and more radical interpretations.

Turner's main contribution centered in his

pronouncement on the significance of the
frontier in American history, a set of ideas
now so familiar that there is no need to re-
prise them. Bolton was the effective dis-
coverer of the Spanish Borderlands. He was a
militant advocate of reconnoitering the actual
terrain where history had been made. He was
also the great protagonist of the hemispheric
approach to the study of the history of the
Americas. The gist of his teaching was the
idea of a broad approach, multinational and,
in the colonial period, multi-imperial. Webb
was a four-time revisionist. In *The Great
Plains* he insisted that the force of the environment was of transcendent importance. In
*Divided We Stand* he cried out against the
economic colonialism pressed down on the
South and the West. In *The Great Frontier*
he reappraised what used to be called the expansion of Europe. "Perpetual Mirage" came
as a tract telling the West it was desert at the
core.

In his lifetime, Turner heard little criticism
of his frontier thesis. But after his death, the
thesis was denounced, attacked, and rejected

by many scholars in and out of the western field. Posthumously, Bolton has been challenged on his contention that the Americas have a common history. In his day, there was little systematic rebuttal, but so far as the nationwide fraternity of scholars was concerned, most of the seed that Bolton scattered fell on stony ground.

Webb's critics did not wait his going. With foundation support, a group of scholars marginal to the western field lit a back-fire against his *Great Plains*. His publisher did his best to suppress Webb's second "idea book." The essay on aridity set many westerners to sputtering. And *The Great Frontier*, by Webb's own calculation, had no prospect of being appreciated until at least 1990.

From their experiences, one might conclude that the way of the historical interpreter or generalizer is hard. And it is. Yet Turner, Bolton, and Webb each intended to be provocative. And their fame and prominence rest far less on their orthodox contributions than on their challenging interpretations and ideas.

# CONTENTS

[xi]

# ILLUSTRATIONS

# TURNER, BOLTON, AND WEBB

*Three Historians of the American Frontier*

Courtesy Henry E. Huntington Library

Frederick Jackson Turner, 1906

*Wilbur R. Jacobs*

# FREDERICK JACKSON TURNER

THE Frederick Jackson Turner papers reveal the problems a great historian had in getting his ideas down on paper. Some writers—Francis Parkman and William Prescott, for instance—were fortunate in possessing literary talents of a high order; indeed, they achieved their renown in large part through their gift of language and evocation.

Research necessary for the completion of this essay was made possible by grants-in-aid from the Henry E. Huntington Library in 1961 and 1964 and by funds allocated by the Committee on Research, University of California, Santa Barbara. An article on Turner published in *The American West*, I (Winter, 1964), 32–35, 78, is based on this longer essay.

[3]

But Turner, though he is capable of admirable lucidity in his essays, and although many of his letters are sprightly and pleasantly conversational in tone, found writing for publication painfully difficult.

The fact is that Turner was a writer by virtue of necessity. Turner's collected papers, his correspondence, research notes, and unpublished essays all reveal that his approach to history was nonliterary, that he sought to borrow from the scientific method what history could use—an approach we recognize as strikingly modern. Turner was preoccupied with the massing of evidence, the sifting of data to reach objective conclusions, and the consideration of theoretical formulations and hypotheses. He was above all interested in the interplay of many varied forces—social, political, cultural, diplomatic, economic, geographical—and absorbed in the task of documenting the evolutionary aspects of this interplay, rather than in depicting the character of a man, the mood of a dramatic historical scene, or the appearance of a place.

More than anyone else, Turner was conscious of his own limitations as a writer. In describing his prospective book on the history of the United States, 1830–50, to publishers, Turner said that he planned to stress "topics like slavery, commerce, interstate migration" which might be expanded into a later book on the era 1850–65. One of his main problems, Turner told his publishers, was dealing with "the narrative side." "It is in narrative history that I am least experienced or (I fear) competent." Turner continued:

And in condensed narrative especially—My strength, or weakness, lies in interpretation, correlation, elucidation of large tendencies to bring out new points of view and in giving a new setting. This appeals to the student who already knows the conventional narrative; but less to the general reader. I get on better (to put it specifically and with reference to my *trade* as a University instructor) in presenting my data to graduates already equipped with a course in American history, than to beginning undergraduates. I'm not a good saga-man.

Turner's unromantic approach to writing and teaching is borne out by notes he made for his last lectures on the history of the West in 1923, the year he retired from Harvard.

"Aspects of the Westward Movement in American History," Turner wrote, involved "a study of selected topics in the history of the West considered as a process rather than an area."

This stress on ideas, the highly intellectual quality of Turner's writings, might perplex some readers of his work on the frontier and the West, for these subjects seem to lend themselves to a dramatic and romantic treatment. But Turner's approach was not romantic, and he considered western development as a complex "process" which needed to be understood in all its details. Writing to Merle Curti after his retirement from Harvard, and after his tenure as a research associate at the Huntington Library in California had begun, Turner made the following comments about the character of his writings:

My work, whether good or bad, can only be correctly judged by noting what American historians and teachers of history (see College & Univ. catalogues of the later eighties) were doing when I began. . . . The attitude toward Western history was at the time largely antiquarian or of the romantic narrative type devoid of the conception of the "West" as a

[6]

Aspects of the Westward Movement in American History.

A study of selected topics in the history of the West considered as a process rather than an area. The movement of the people from the Atlantic coast. the advance of the frontier into the free lands of the wilderness; the influence of regional geography; the formation of new sections; the effect upon the eastern states, economically, and their relation to the diplomatic history politically and socially, will be discussed.

The work of the class will consist of readings outlined in Turner and Merk, List of Readings in the History of the West (1923), and F. J. Turner, Frontier in American History; Lobeck's Physiographic Diagram of the United States and small outline maps of the United States will also be used.

Five hours a week.

The first three weeks of the course will be given by Professor Turner, to about 1840, and the second three weeks by Dr Merk.

"... the West considered as a process ..."
Turner's classroom notes of 1923, the year he retired from Harvard

moving process—modifying the East, and involving economic, political and social factors.

And again:

As you know, the "West" with which I dealt, was a *process* rather than a fixed geographical region: it began with the Atlantic Coast; and it emphasized the way in which the East colonized the West, and how the "West," as it stood at any given period affected the development and ideas of the older areas to the East. In short, the "frontier" was taken as the "thin red line" that recorded the *dynamic* element in American history up to recent times.

Turner's "West," then, was by his own explanation not the golden one, but, as near as he was capable of making it, the historical process of the real and changing West. Turner was more interested in veracity of thought than in any "artistic" verities or literary "unities." And his essays, as a result, are not stylistic tours de force, but clear, unadorned historical interpretations, the product of a logical and questioning mind. "So far as my style goes," Turner wrote Frederick Merk, "it was really an outcome of my own earnest interest in the subject rather than an attempt to emphasize literary form."

## Frederick Jackson Turner

Turner's concept of an historical "process," involving, as it does, continuous changes in time and a constantly shifting kaleidoscope of interrelated forces, is a matter much too vast and mobile to be grasped easily. It is incomparably more difficult to describe and analyze on paper than a static picture, or even a series of static pictures. The process with which Turner dealt, and which he struggled to get down on paper so it could be understood by others, comprised at least four separate but related movements. These included, as he wrote in an unpublished essay,

[1] the spread of settlement steadily westward, and [2] all the economic, social, and political changes involved in the existence of a belt of free land at the edge of settlement; [3] the continual settling of successive belts of land; [4] the evolution of these successive areas of settlement through various stages of backwoods life, ranching, pioneer farming, scientific farming, and manufacturing life.

Turner believed that the history of the process of westward expansion must include not only an account of the western occupation of the land and the accompanying evolution of society from pioneer life to an urban manufacturing society but, as he said, "all the economic, social and political changes" at the edge of settlement as these various "Wests" went through a "process" of social evolution. The most gifted and facile writer would have found it an arduous task to write history of such density and complexity!*

Had Turner's work been less original, the obstacles in the way of published results would have been less formidable. But his was an independent and creative effort, and he lacked accumulations of background material and published documents which those who followed him have used with profit. Turner's lifetime accumulation of research notes, housed in dozens of bulging file drawers, was not simply an eccentric luxury or the results of a neurotic habit of "a glutton for data." These files were the tools necessary to build the new history. Although Turner modestly

* Avery Craven in a recent letter to the author comments on this point. "I knew him," Dr. Craven writes of Turner, "both as a student and as a companion at the Huntington Library the last year of his life, and had many long talks with him in that mellow year. The trouble was that his conception of 'what is history,' was so complex that neither he nor anyone else could or can do much with it beyond the essay form."

declined to claim for himself the title of
founder of the so-called new history, his
contribution to it was probably greater than
that of any other historian of his generation.
When he wrote to his publishers in 1919 re-
garding the advertising of his book of essays,
*The Frontier in American History,* which
was about to be published, Turner said, "I
prefer not to enter any claims, either to a *'new
history,'* or anything of that sort, but let my
work stand for what it is, & what it was at
the dates when the successive contributions
appeared. And above all I don't want to seem
to advertise myself. . . ."

Convinced that most American historians
had distorted accounts of the times they pro-
fessed to treat, Turner believed he had no
real alternative but to take on the almost
overwhelming job of reinterpreting his country's history. "What I was dealing with,"
Turner wrote, "was . . . the American character of democracy as compared with that of
Europe or of European philosophers." He
complained that few historians had written
about the American West except as "annex-

ation-of-territory history." When he began his researches Turner perceived that America "beyond the Alleghenies, was almost virgin soil, and that the *frontier process* began with the coast; and that the South also—indeed all the sections—needed restudy objectively." Turner believed that the only earlier historian who successfully related "economic and social data to American history" was Henry Adams, who

does much in the first volume of his history with that sort of thing, though he doesn't do it in my way. The tendency was to deal with such topics in one or two separate chapters and then turn, without knitting the two together, to political and diplomatic history. I have tried to keep the relations steadily in mind, but it isn't an easy job, and the effort [here Turner shows himself conscious of his low literary productivity] is sometimes conducive to unwritten books!

Turner was, of course, aware that in his attempts to counteract the static histories of the past, to present a new and infinitely more subtle account of the American experience, he was in danger of being misunderstood. The true breadth of his treatment was too often ignored; "undue emphasis," he thought, had been placed upon his interest in Western history. Critics often failed to grasp, he wrote in 1925 to Arthur M. Schlesinger, that his theory of the frontier and the "process" of westward expansion was an attempt to show how "the interior" was "a necessary element in an understanding of the America of the time." This "interior" Turner saw as "a modifying element," a "mixing bowl," and as "a parent region for much of the mountain states and the [Pacific] Coast." Turner thought of the new "Wests," in various stages of social and economic evolution, as colonies of the East, and he sometimes referred to them collectively as America's "interior." The actual frontier, however, had to be distinguished from the westward movement as a "process." "Of course [the] Frontier and [the] West are not identical," Turner wrote in one of his letters to Schlesinger, "but I used [the] Frontier as (so to speak) the barometric line that recorded the advance of settlement, the creation of new Wests, not merely as the area of Indian fighting, vigilantes, annexations, etc." Similarly, in writing to Carl Becker he pointed out that his self-assumed task of treating precisely those areas most neglected by historians could be easily misinterpreted:

Although my work has laid stress upon two aspects of American history—the frontier and the sections (in the sense of geographical regions, or provinces . . .), I do not think of myself as primarily either a western historian, or a human geographer. I have stressed these two factors, because it seemed to me that they had been neglected, but fundamentally I have been interested in the inter-relations of economics, politics, sociology, culture in general, with the geographic factors, in explaining the United States of today by means of its history thus broadly taken. Perhaps this is one of the many reasons why I have not been more voluminous!

With some justification Turner objected to his conception of the frontier being used "as a man of straw to be pummeled." It is not surprising that he roused himself from a sickbed in December, 1931, shortly before his death, to dictate a long letter to a critic who implied that he was guilty of "spreading an error" by implying that the frontier "ended in

1890." "Of course," Turner wrote, "the frontier did not end in 1890 . . . 'with a bang.' . . . However, the importance of the frontier movement as a large factor in American history did reach its close about that time, and an examination of legislation, economic development, social traits, etc., would make this clear."

Turner disliked the oversimplification involved in being labeled, or "tagged," one thing or another. His concept of history was so broad that he even objected to being classified as "a Western historian." When a distinguished scholar told him that he behaved like a sociologist, not a historian, Turner answered, "I didn't care what I was called, so long as I was left to try to ascertain the truth, and the relation of facts to cause and effect in my own way." Turner naturally enough objected to the idea, voiced by both Charles A. Beard and Arthur M. Schlesinger, that he stressed an economic interpretation of history. Writing to Schlesinger in 1922, Turner said that he did not know if his frontier studies represented "fundamentally an economic interpretation." "There is in this country," he continued, "such an interrelation of ideals, economic interest, frontier advance (or recession, if you prefer), and regional geography, that it isn't easy to separate them." While Turner believed that his essays on the West showed an "appreciation of the economic changes," they were, he wrote, "more related to the influence of free lands and the frontier in the large sense." "The truth is," he added, "that I found it necessary to hammer pretty hard and pretty steadily on the frontier idea to 'get it in,' as a corrective to the kind of thinking I found some thirty years ago and less." Furthermore, he hoped to spend his later years adding a "companion piece (the Section) to the Frontier." If he lived, Turner concluded in this interesting letter to Schlesinger, he would "attempt a coordination of these old and new viewpoints in a general sketch of our history, emphasizing the dynamics rather than the statics: the genetic element, and the flow of it all."

The task that Turner set for himself, then, was to win acceptance for new viewpoints

and to combine them in a dynamic history
which stressed interrelationships and what he
called the "genetic element." He was well
aware that the "frontier process" which he
sought to describe was related to the other
processes of American history such as "the
evolution of sectionalism," "the evolution of
political institutions," "the evolution of a
composite, non-English nationality, the industrial transformations," "the slavery strug-
gle and the negro suffrage problem." Beyond
this, not only did Turner see that his theory
might have applications in countries other
than in his own—in Russia and in South
America for example—but he recognized that
the history of all the world might be considered in terms of the "processes" of history.

The "frontier" process [Turner declared in a letter
to Carl Becker] is one which applies to certain portions of Old World history, as well as to that of the
New, and sometime it will be worked out thus. And
beyond all this is the conception of history as a complex of all the social sciences. The conception of
the One-ness of the thing. As you intimate, this is a
rather paralyzing conception. I didn't consciously
fashion it as a guide book to begin with (and I can't

[17]

claim authorship of it)! but it does help to know that these subjects are tied together and to deal with a phase of the whole, realizing it is only a phase.

All his life Turner worked in orderly fashion preparing the ground for his reinterpretation of history, a task of almost incredible complexity. A never-ending accumulation of data swelled his wooden filing cases and cardboard 3 x 5 filing boxes. The contents of the files was the raw material which it was the job of the historian to digest, for Turner did not suppose that the piling up of raw facts and statistics made history. We find him cautioning a former student of his, Arthur H. Buffinton, who is teaching in a small college and preparing a dissertation: "I am prone to believe that you are still influenced by your early, student, ideal of setting forth *all* the detailed facts, with which I always quarrelled with you," Turner wrote. "But it is your mutton, and I don't mean to interfere with its cooking! Only I should like to eat the dish before I quit eating!"

Turner's constant emphasis on evaluating source materials stemmed from his belief that

a central idea should emerge from the survey
of the data. He warned Buffinton against letting detail interfere with over-all interpretation, telling him, "Let the thoroughness of
detailed investigation appear clearly enough,
especially in footnote citations and illustra-
tions, and bibliography, to make it clear that
the 'grind' has preceded the grist."

This method of evaluating and selecting
data carries with it obvious dangers, for so
much must depend on the investigator's abil-
ity to weigh and assess his material, and
Turner was well aware of the difficulty of
achieving the requisite degree of objectivity.
Indeed, he believed that "no historian could
be absolutely free from personal equation,"
although by choosing to present only facts
one could steer fairly clear of the dangers of
imposing one's own conscious or unconscious
biases. But this, obviously, is not the job of
the responsible historian. In his classes, Turner
wrote, he attempted "to preach the importance of reaching conclusions on relative importance of facts, and the need of dealing
with relations, the causal element and with

results, as the only way to avoid mere dumping of brick and mortar for another's use."

While it was possible to provide his students with some training in the process of evaluating data, it was less easy to provide them with the training in related fields which would enable them to carry on investigations on the broad lines recommended by Turner. In truth, Turner wrote, "the man who does general history on these lines must indeed be a genius; but with some equipment in the other social fields and some knowledge of the scientific method and tools he should be able to consult the special works intelligently so as to proceed not too narrowly in the orientation of his subject and the development of it." The problem that is raised here, that of the extent of the knowledge necessary to pursue all the facets of history, led Turner to the recognition that some limitation was not only possible, but probably necessary. "I don't object to rather rigid limitations of a study," he wrote, "if it is done expressly, and with the consciousness of the limitations."

Although willing to advise students to

limit the range of their inquiry, Turner found himself less willing to submit his own work to barriers of his own making. In his treatment of the leading figures in *Rise of the New West,* for example, Turner has considered a whole range of factors which may control the actions and policies of statesmen —personal, religious, climatic, and geographical. In one of his unpublished essays, Turner pointed out that factors like "inherited ideas [and] spiritual factors often triumph over material interests." The statesman had to represent both ideals and interests of his section, and "not seldom the ideals grow out of the interests."

In one of his letters to Merle Curti, Turner explained how he thought a statesman's policies embodying the ideals and interests of his constituents might best be studied, and in this explanation we again see Turner's unromantic and analytical approach to history. Turner told Curti that to see how a leader was forced to shape and revise his views one would do well to study the influences of his environment, of his society, of his political opposition, and of the support of "lesser men," rather than to turn to the minutiae of biography. Although he believed "personality and accident play a very real part in history," Turner wrote Curti that these factors were probably "exaggerated by historians and by biographers." On one of his file cards Turner outlined his approach to the study of a leader. Under "personality," Turner notes that he intends to look into biographies, newspapers, magazines, records of speeches, votes in Congress, correspondence, as well as "to examine works of contemporaries." Below these notations Turner lists his intention of making an "estimate of character, environment, policy —(development)—" and estimate the statesman's "Place in Am[erican] history." History, Turner believed, was neither the " 'lengthened shadow of the great man,' nor the result of economic determinism in which the leader doesn't count." What was most important, was "to gather details . . . to dig deeply—and then reject immaterial or subordinate details." Yet Turner cautioned, "This process of elimination . . . cannot well be done safely until the field has been surveyed in sufficient detail to reach a conclusion on the important and unimportant.''

In Turner's *Rise of the New West,* leaders such as Henry Clay, John Quincy Adams, and John C. Calhoun can be recognized as spokesmen for their society. As Turner's large file of 3 x 5 cards demonstrates, their portraits were based on a vast mass of data, filed under subject headings ''physiography,'' ''transportation,'' ''canals,'' ''raw products,'' ''immigration,'' ''nullification,'' or by chronology, month by month, year by year. In drawer 4 of his 3 x 5 card file, Turner has only a few cards on such figures as Henry Clay, Daniel Webster, John Calhoun, John Quincy Adams, John Marshall, and other statesmen of the era, but his method of collecting information indicates clearly that he considered the forces which make and influence a man more important for the historian than an account of his life.

In spite of this methodical approach to his work, writing, for Turner, was a hardship. ''He has never been able to 'compose' except when under the lash," one commentator says of him. "Writing his own stuff is agony to him; and his constitution, despite his ruddy complexion, has never been robust." *Rise of the New West* would probably never have been completed without the urging of Albert Bushnell Hart, and for Turner it was a dreadful experience. In the first place, the problems of accumulating sufficient data for his published works were enormous. For Turner there was the additional difficulty that he lost himself in his investigations and was unwilling to put a stop to them, that he constantly felt himself insufficiently prepared.

"Some of my own difficulty in publishing," he writes to Buffinton, "arises from my realization of the many factors essential to a fundamental treatment, and a dislike to issue a partial survey." Another reason for his relatively few publications was the enormous scope of his investigations which led him into areas not previously thought of as the domain of the historian. Turner's breadth of view was, as he told Becker, "one of the many reasons why I have not been more voluminous." And, of course, Turner was faced with the mammoth job of evaluating his data, sifting his material, and arranging it so that the complexity of the historical forces at work was clearly set before the reader, allowing him to examine it, rather than be swamped by it. As Fulmer Mood has pointed out in his searching essay on Turner as a historical thinker,

the literary problems which presented themselves to Turner [in writing *Rise of the New West*] were difficult in the extreme. He had at the outset to describe and characterize each of the several sections that composed the Union. In these accounts he had to present a truthful general picture, well-rounded sociologically, and at the same time contrive to give a sense of the development locally, of the movement of history within the particular section. . . . National history, as studied in Congressional action and presidential policy, came . . . to have coordinate interest and importance with the internal history of the sections. And underneath all, the strong tide of nascent democracy was shown silently on the upsweep, moving toward the political victory of Jackson in 1828.

In one of his unpublished essays, Turner called attention to another factor that plagued him in writing, that of achieving a sense of historical proportion, or avoiding an "improper perspective." Turner compared historical writing to describing a large animal, say an elephant. What might do harm, Turner maintained, was lack of perspective or outright omissions, which he believed were worse than defects caused by inaccurate statements. "If I aim to describe an elephant, and give only an account of his feet," Turner declared, "alleging at the same time that this constitutes the elephant, the microscopic accuracy and keenness of criticism of these organs will not atone for the failure to speak of the rest of the animal." But Turner was not satisfied in commenting on the elephantine problem of obtaining proper historical proportion. When one spoke of the feet or the trunk of an elephant, Turner said, they cannot be seen "in a state of rest." "Unless I describe them in action and in growth," Turner wrote, "I have failed to describe the organ." Lack of perspective is what marred the work of historians like Hermann Von Holst, according to Turner. They were unable to see the whole, dynamic body of American history because they immersed themselves in bodies of static detail.

But although Turner was ready to criticize those historians whose work did not reach the high level that he set for his profession, he was in fact the most modest of men. He was painfully aware of his own shortcomings as a historian and eager to acknowledge his indebtedness to others—particularly to William F. Allen whose lectures on medieval history Turner attended when he was at Wisconsin, and to Woodrow Wilson under whom he studied at Johns Hopkins. Furthermore, he was eager to disclaim any praise which might come to him as the creator of the frontier theory. Calling it "my intellectual first born," Turner wrote William E. Dodd "it would have been more than an unpleasant thing for me to contend for the parentage . . . to try to claim any exclusive property in an idea that would have evolved from the nature of growing American consciousness itself. . . ." Indeed, Turner's concept of history was far from being that of an egotist. He saw that the new interpretation of

## Wilbur R. Jacobs

American history would have to be the work of the scholarly community; it was patently impossible for one man to treat all of history in the complex fashion that complex history demanded. He was only one of many, and he put great effort into making sure that there would be others to continue his work.

As a teacher, Turner was completely successful, which may seem surprising in the light of his insistence on painstaking scholarship and extreme accuracy and objectivity—virtues which the young are not always eager to practice. But Turner was able to sugar the pill of the discipline he was teaching with the charm of his own personality. The interest which he took in his student's work convinced the student of its importance. Turner "radiated," according to his intimate friend and disciple Ulrich B. Phillips, a kind of eagerness which became "a large element in his glorious quality as a teacher." Phillips commented on the copious notes which Turner took

from reports being read by students in his seminar. This gave the youngsters an impression that what they were doing was immensely worthwhile. His eagerness is of the contagious kind. He has been very fond of quoting and appropriating Basil Gildersleeve's self-characterization as not an instructor but a radiator. No one has been more justly entitled to the term. He has not so much written books as made a school and created a tradition. But the best of this is that his disciples are not content (the good ones) to walk in his steps, but are eager to blaze paths of their own.

Turner's congenial relationship with his "research students" is perhaps best illustrated by what he told Carl Becker in 1928: "As I grow older the more I realize how much the companionship of my research students has meant to me. Not the *educational* aspect, not the teaching, but the companionship of men out on the adventure after historical truth, and incidentally the desire to help them to outstrip their guide in finding the trail and the new horizons."

Turner's interest in his students was not confined to the work they did in his classroom or seminar. Although he sometimes allowed them to suffer "salutary neglect" in "hopeful expectation," he was always prepared to give them advice and criticism, even though the time thus consumed left still less for his own work. To Arthur H. Buffinton, for instance, he not only wrote detailed suggestions for the preparation of his dissertation, but sent some friendly suggestions for the conduct of his career, urging him to complete his thesis as soon as posible: "You are no longer so young that you can remain without a book to your credit without doing yourself injustice. If the project above will hasten it by getting you out of the stage of doctoral candidacy into that of writer, I will do all I can to assist! 'Come on in! The water's fine!' " At about the same time, we find Turner encouraging Buffinton to withstand the trials of a young teacher:

I have taught general history and medieval history, and English history, and recent modern history, and elocution, and have run a correspondence course in Oriental history! So I know some of your trials. But such things do broaden the view, if you live through them, and better men than either of us have been all the better for having occupied a settee instead of a chair. Cheer up, and take Dr. Walter Camp's Daily Dozen Exercises (price 10 cents).

Turner assumed the twofold task of training young men for the work before them and of leaving the results of his own investigations in printed form. In theory, at least, Turner stressed the second half of the obligation: "We must build foundations, and furnish *real* bricks for those who come after us, and profit by our mistakes and half sight—and there is a real danger of merely thinking 'by and large.' "

It is small wonder, considering the vastness of Turner's chosen task (involving a conception of history that even Carl Becker found "rather paralyzing"), that Turner was sometimes depressed at his failure to produce more in the form of polished printed results. "In truth," Turner wrote, "there is no single key to American history. In history, as in science, we are learning that a complex result is the outcome of the interplay of many forces. Simple explanations fail to meet the case."

The task of writing the new history, taking the broad Turnerean view in interpreting our past, was surely an undertaking of the first magnitude. Turner, in giving special attention to one important phase of "general"

American history, was fascinated by the great mass of human action on the frontier and in the West. He saw American society clothed in its spiritual and material Old World inheritance, a captive of customs, suddenly thrust into an infinitely complex environmental and social setting on the raw frontier. It was here that the "bonds of custom" were broken by the frontier process of social change.

With the greatest earnestness, Turner sought to understand the relationship between the confused memory of the past and the intricate reality of the present. Despite the magnitude of the problem, he felt an obligation to leave the results of his investigations in printed form. In speaking of his goal Turner wrote: "Mine, if I have any, has been largely unconscious . . . the search beyond the skyline for new truth, and the use of such methods of getting there as immediate needs & resources permitted."

While occupied in a lifelong search for this "new truth," Turner seems to have acquired a feeling of guilt at his failure to leave more

for later historians. But we, looking back on
his life, can see that his publications were held
in check by precisely those qualities which
made him a historian of such enduring value
—his awareness of the enormous scope and
complexity of history which precluded rash
and casual judgments, and his strong sense of
responsibility to his profession which caused
him to busy himself so magnificently with its
future practitioners, his students—represented
by Merle Curti and Carl Becker—who became leaders of a great host of distinguished
disciples. But a critic of Turner rather than
one of his admirers expressed most precisely
the debt which our present generation of historians owes its great predecessor: "It was Mr.
Turner," Charles A. Beard wrote in a letter
of 1928, "who led in putting history on a
scientific plane." Turner himself wrote in one
of his last letters, in 1931, that he had attempted "to deal with economic, political,
and social subjects in relation to American
history and geography and by a method of
using the sciences and scientific method. I can-

not claim to be a scientist," Turner concluded, "but I have realized the importance of understanding their point of view and methods."

# Note on Sources

In the course of a long preoccupation with Frederick Jackson Turner's writings and his papers at the Huntington Library, at Harvard, at the University of Wisconsin, at Princeton, and at other document repositories, I have contracted intellectual debts that are difficult to repay. I am particularly indebted to the brilliant essayists on Turner: Carl Becker, Merle Curti, Fulmer Mood, Avery Craven, Ray Billington, and Norman Harper. Most of all, however, this paper, which is part of a book-length study on Turner's thought and his significance as a teacher and historian, is based on what he said about himself, especially in his later years. This information was culled from a large mass of Tur-

ner's unpublished essays and lectures, his re-
search materials, and his correspondence with
his publishers, with Carl Becker, Merle Curti,
Frederick Merk, Arthur M. Schlesinger, Arthur H. Buffinton, Max Farrand, Isaiah
Bowman, William E. Dodd, Charles A.
Beard, Edgar Eugene Robinson, Harry Elmer
Barnes, James Harvey Robinson, and others.
The large portion of this manuscript material
is described in "The Frederick Jackson Turner
Papers in the Huntington Library," by Ray
A. Billington and Wilbur R. Jacobs, *Arizona
and the West*, II (Spring, 1960), 73–77. In
his letters Turner sometimes referred his students to his American Historical Association
presidential address, "Social Forces in American History" (published in *The Frontier in
American History*, New York, 1920, pp.
311–34), for what he called, "my general
ideas of the scope and methods."

# Selected Bibliography

## FREDERICK JACKSON TURNER

---

### BOOKS

*The Frontier in American History*. New York: Henry Holt, 1920; Holt, Rinehart, & Winston, 1962.

This collection, carefully chosen by Turner, includes several of his most influential essays that helped shape the basic interpretations of American history. They include the thesis that provoked the controversy over the frontier hypothesis, "The Significance of the Frontier in American History" (1893), and "Social Forces in American History" (1910), an address synthesizing Turner's main interpretations. The new edition has a foreword by Ray A. Billington.

*Rise of the New West, 1819–29*. New York: Harpers, 1906; Collier Books, 1962.

Printed by Harpers (1906) as a volume in the American Nation Series; republished (1963) with foreword by Ray A. Billington.

## Frederick Jackson Turner

*The Significance of Sections in American History.*
New York: Henry Holt, 1932; Gloucester, Mass.:
Peter Smith, 1959.

This second book of essays appeared posthumously and was awarded the Pulitzer prize. The essay "Problems in American History" provides the introduction to "The Significance of the Section in American History" which analyzes the whole problem of sectionalism.

*The Early Writings of Frederick Jackson Turner.*
Compiled by Everett E. Edwards with an introductory essay by Fulmer Mood. Madison: University of Wisconsin Press, 1938.

Turner's intellectual development may be traced through a study of his early essays which appear in this volume: "The Character and Influence of the Fur Trade in Wisconsin" (1889);* "The Significance of History" (1891); "Problems in American History" (1892); "The Significance of the Frontier in American History" (1893). The book also contains a virtually complete bibliography of Turner's writings.

*The Frontier and Section.* Ray A. Billington, ed. Englewood Cliffs, N.J.: Prentice-Hall, 1961.

Contains three of the essays listed above (1891, 1892, and 1893); also "The Significance of the Section in American History."

---

* Turner's doctoral dissertation, "The Character and Influence of the Indian Trade in Wisconsin: A Study of the Trading Post as an Institution," first published in the *Johns Hopkins University Studies in Historical and Political Science,* IX (Baltimore, 1891), 541–615.

# Wilbur R. Jacobs

*The United States, 1830–1850: The Nation and Its Sections.* New York: Henry Holt, 1935.

>  Introduction by Avery Craven. Posthumously published. A remarkable history evolving out of interpretations set forth in early essays. Since it was partly dictated, this book lacks much of the stylistic vigor of Turner's other works.

*Frederick Jackson Turner's Legacy: Unpublished Writings in American History.* Edited with an introduction by Wilbur R. Jacobs. Huntington Library, San Marino, Calif., 1965.

>  Contains previously unpublished writings: the complexity of history, American social history, the city, education and democracy, varying themes on the frontier and the section. Also included is Turner's revised version of one of his most significant essays, "The Development of American Society" (1908).

*The Historical World of Frederick Jackson Turner: Selected Correspondence.* Edited with an introduction by Wilbur R. Jacobs. Yale University, New Haven, Connecticut, in press.

>  Nearly one hundred letters to fellow historians and students, an autobiography in the form of letters.

## PERIODICAL

"Notes on the Westward Movement, California, and the Far West," W. R. Jacobs, ed. *Southern California Quarterly,* XLVI (June, 1964), 161–68.

## *Frederick Jackson Turner*

Turner compiled these notes in 1927–29, revealing that in retrospect his view of the frontier theory was considerably altered by his residence in Southern California as research associate at the Huntington Library.

Herbert Eugene Bolton

*John W. Caughey*

---

# HERBERT
# EUGENE
# BOLTON

---

WHEN I first met Herbert Eugene Bolton he was in his prime. In any activity or profession, "prime" means the time when energy and experience are in the equilibrium that yields peak efficiency and output. From historian to historian the time may vary. For most of us it probably comes sooner, but for Bolton I am prepared to date it in the years when he was fifty-five, fifty-six, and fifty-seven. Here is part of the evidence.

He then held the office of director of the Bancroft Library. He was chairman of the

[41]

history department at the University of California at Berkeley. His teaching stint called for lecturing twice a week to a thousand undergraduates studying the history of the Americas. Three times a week he lectured to a couple of hundred upperclassmen and graduates on the history of the West. Thursday nights a score of graduate students gathered at his round table, almost every one of them working under his direction toward the M.A. or Ph.D.

To the seminar in my three years, he brought many evidences of his dedication to research—new books or articles by some of "his boys"; finished copies of *Arredondo's Historical Proof* and *The Debatable Land*, page proofs of *Palou's New California*, galleys of *Crespi, Missionary Explorer*, and parts of the manuscript of *Anza*.

Because he haunted his study and operated on the open-door policy, access to him was easy—provided one was willing to climb the stairs to the fourth floor of the library. In my second year as teaching assistant I gained a further entree. I was chosen as his map man, which meant I had a standing appointment to drop in an hour before his lecture to find which two or three oversize maps he wanted hung and in what arrangement. I always found him jotting notes for the lecture, but my coming was usually the signal for a conversation break, a Bolton institution.

Aside from class and seminar, his study was the only place where I ever saw him. Still, he was a very open person. He put himself into everything that he did. To illustrate a technique in research or a problem of assessing evidence, he liked best of all to relate some experience or achievement of his own. I thought I knew him well, but I must admit that my understanding was clarified and corrected as late as 1962 when a reminiscent account by his elder brother Frederick appeared in *Arizona and the West*. Bolton used to say that he had no need to play golf because he had plenty of exercise when he was young. I took that as a joke, as of course it was, but Frederick spells out how much toil and labor Herbert had to put in as a youth and a young man.

## John W. Caughey

Besides being a straightforward and uncomplicated person, Bolton had found the line of work that he wanted to pursue—the particular kind of history and the particular kind of teaching and research—and he was applying himself full tilt. For this assignment he had tremendous enthusiasm, which spread out to embrace others—especially his students—who were engaged with him in this great adventure. Observers from the sidelines occasionally said that he was too self-centered. All recognized his diligence in going to the sources, his alertness in uncovering new documents, and his unflagging devotion to his chosen task. It was not just the long hours he worked, past midnight night after night; it was also that he let nothing divert him.

His methods were simple yet demanding. He was one of the pioneers in the discovery and the opening of foreign archives materials on American history. "I am an American historian," he said in the first sentence of one speech, "and therefore I do my research in foreign archives." He meant Mexico, Spain, the Vatican, the Jesuit Archives, France, The Netherlands, and so on.

The Sabuaganas

One of the Tribes Escalante had
planned to visit on his way were the
Sabuaganas in the northwest. It will
be remembered that on August 19, when
struggling through Gypsum
Canyon on Dolores River, the travelers
were undecided whether to follow a
trail they had come upon or "go
back a short distance and take a
road that leads to the Sabuaganas". To
settle the debate they resorted to
pious gambling. Casting lots between
the two trails they drew
the one leading to the Sabuaganas
and decided to follow it until they
reached that tribe. Four days later,
at Fuente de la Guia, in Tabeguache
country, when Escalante asked his
new guide about the Tabeguaches,
Muhuaches, and Sabuaganas, he

A typical manuscript page from Bolton's writings

## John W. Caughey

He took to the trails. He was not content merely to pore over the manuscripts and old maps. He preferred to revisit the scene, to confirm or correct the locations, and to let the geography contribute directly to his understanding of the history he was studying. Usually thereafter he had to reconstruct the maps as well as the narrative. In respects other than geographical he tried to put himself in the position of the people he was studying, whether they were Spaniards, Frenchmen, Englishmen, or Indians. I cannot picture him beating a drum for integration, yet a cardinal belief of his was that people of all races and nationalities are very much alike. He delighted in exploding the stereotypes in which the Spaniards had been cast. He sought help from ethnologists as well as geographers and from other specialists where appropriate. From his own researches he was able to contribute significant data for ethnological study.

How he met the obligations as director of the Bancroft Library and chairman of the history department was not visible to me as a graduate student. He cannot have allowed either to consume much of his time.

His performance as a teacher I have never seen paralleled. He was a teaching machine, a one-man assembly line, a taxpayers' dream of efficiency in the degree factory. Each semester he brought twelve hundred or more undergraduates one course nearer to graduation. It was a poor commencement when his masters did not number ten or a dozen and his doctors four or five.

The paradox was that he did not seem to be a good lecturer. He was neither dramatic nor spectacular. He did not try to entertain, nor was he truly eloquent. Instead, he offered a down-to-earth exposition, a straightforward narrative, together with his observations on the meaning. Clearly he was talking out of solid knowledge. More important, he showed his keenness for the grand development that was his subject and his zest for the study. He achieved a contagion of interest in the pursuit and recapture of a fleeting past.

In his graduate seminar he was even more successful in communicating his consuming interest in the study of history. Bolton never thought of his seminar as a place of instruction in the mechanics of historical research.

He frankly said that he left that sort of teaching to his colleagues. They, by their own choice or otherwise, carried on a quite different pedagogy. Louis Paetow offered a seminar in research method. Eugene I. McCormac ran a colloquium with oral reports on assigned fractions of a common topic. Charles E. Chapman made his seminar a bull ring of criticism, the sharper the better.

Bolton used his seminar as a forum where his thesis and dissertation writers read chapters, or what they hoped were chapters, in the offering that would partially fulfill a degree requirement. In any semester the subject matter might spread over several centuries and over the whole Boltonian range from Alaska to the West Indies and from the Great Basin to Patagonia. As Bolton students we were supposed to be more or less prepared to understand. In fact, a virtue of Bolton's wide-ranging seminar was that his Latin American specialists received broad exposure to the history of the West and his Western Americanists got a grounding in the history of Latin America. The quality, of course, varied. Some of the offerings were inadequately researched, poorly organized, or badly written. Bolton, nevertheless, almost always steered the comment to some element in the performance that was eligible for praise, even if it were only the map or other exhibit material accompanying the report.

Opinion differed on how Bolton came to have this penchant for praise. By mid-career it was a fixed characteristic. He interpreted his role as mentor to mean that first of all he gave encouragement. It bespoke more confidence in human performance and less pleasure in fault-finding than most of us have. Bolton carried this same attitude over to book reviewing, usually declining to write a review, and enjoying the task only when he could bestow undiluted applause. In choice of topics for his own research he also favored what he could extol. He preferred success stories, heroes rather than villains.

His seminar method aided his volume output of M.A.'s and Ph.D.'s. The bulk of his advising and supervising was accomplished right in the seminar; some of it, as should be, by the other students present. He used also one factory device. He liked to find sets of subjects for investigation. One such category was federal relations, on which he had a whole battery of students at work; another was Spanish Louisiana; still another, missions and missionaries. I fell into two of these programs, with a thesis on early federal relations with New Mexico and a dissertation in the Spanish Louisiana dispensation.

None of these group attacks has the fame that attaches to William A. Dunning's Reconstruction seminar. There the time span was limited, the states only eleven in number, and the definition primarily political. Federal relations by contrast is an open-end investment. Bolton never had enough hands to encompass it all, nor am I sure that he was interested in pursuing it beyond the early phases. For his seminar the device of related topics was a clear help; it strengthened the seminar as a proving ground, and fitted in with Bolton's method of encouragement unlimited.

Because it is illustrative of much that I have remarked about him, particularly his feeling toward his students and the adventure of learning in which he and they were engaged, I insert a letter dated February 21, 1933, shortly after he had served his term of office as president of the American Historical Association. The volumes referred to are the *Festschrift* of 1932. The Spanish phrase that recurs translates lamely as "farther on"; to him it had more the quality of "Onward, onward!"

My dear Caughey:

I feel most apologetic for not telling you before this how deeply I appreciate your part in the presentation volumes prepared by my students for the Toronto meeting of the American Historical Association. The idea was most generous of them, and a tribute which I prize more highly than I can express.

As you well know, there is no phase of my work that I value so much as my association with my students. It is with them that I find my most satisfactory fellowship. Young men and women are open minded and forward looking. I am an optimist. I like to teach because I believe young men and women worth teaching. A pessimist in the teaching profession must be essentially dishonest, pretending to do something he does not believe in.

The presentation volumes are not only an evidence of the generosity and the loyalty of my students, but

[51]

are also a substantial contribution to the history of New Spain and the Anglo-American West. I have read with great interest and profit your "Alexander McGillivray." It is excellent and I thank you for it. I have always learned from my students vastly more than I ever taught them.

Every monograph in the two volumes contains a nugget quarried from the rich mine which we have prospected together, and every one will serve as a lead or a hunch to other prospectors. Each nugget suggests further adventure in the same direction, for who knows what lies hidden? The pioneer had the advantage of the romance which is born of uncertainty which is another name for boundless possibility, and thus he made hard work a thrilling pursuit *más allá*. The scholar is fortunate if he too can wear glasses tinged with the romance of hope-inspiring uncertainty. In scholarship as in all phases of life it is more blessed to be hopefully on the way than to arrive. And the best of it is that nobody, in his own view, ever arrives, so if he is an optimist he can always be hopefully on the way.

With deep gratitude, and with sincere good wishes for your prosperity and your happiness, I am

Your fellow heir to the treasures of the past, hidden somewhere *más allá*.

[signed] Herbert E. Bolton

Bolton never claimed to be a great philosopher or a deep thinker. He did boast that he had hit upon two or three majestic ideas. One was that history is best observed and best understood by reaching beyond the confines of a single nation. In his day, colonial American history was almost always studied by projecting into the past the boundaries within which the United States started and studying merely that fraction of English colony-planting.

Bolton's move to Texas may have broadened his horizons; his summers in the Mexican archives certainly did so. In 1920 *The Colonization of North America,* written in collaboration with T. M. Marshall, encompassed the multinational multi-imperial efforts affecting the entire continent to 1800. Perhaps better suited for reference use than for reading, this sturdy compendium tabulates a vast array of actions in the European expansion into this continent.

That same year Bolton offered a new course on the history of the Americas, North and South. For it he added a second continent and undertook to cover from Columbus to the present. In point of fact this second part of the contract was not altogether fulfilled. Bolton was a colonialist at heart. He did not turn to the American Revolution and the Wars of Independence until the second semester, and in the national history he was most interested in the colonial-like parts, such as the westward expansion of the United States. He and his class usually found that the second semester disappeared about 1890.

Partly on this account, his United States history colleagues at Berkeley were never content with History 8 as the one lower-division offering in American history. That is another story; which, however, illustrates a barrier that has stood in the way of the spread of the hemisphere course. There have been other handicaps—not enough Bolton-trained and indoctrinated men to staff it in all our colleges; disinclination in some quarters to appoint such nonconformists; the lack, for many years, of a suitable textbook for the course; and prolonged argument in the profession on the irrelevant issue of hemispheric unity, or, as sometimes phrased, Do the Americas have a common history? Bolton, it is true, maintained that there was unity of the sort that rises above the many languages, many nations, many cultures of Europe and that justifies an over-all view of the history of that subcontinent. This concept of the hemispheric view is the one Bolton selected for development in his presidential address to the American Historical Association in 1932, "The Epic of Greater America."

The other concept for which Bolton is best known is that of the Spanish borderlands. He could have included the Banda Oriental (Uruguay), the Guaraní Missions, Paraguay, Tucumán, and southern Chile. His primary reference was to the northern marches of Spanish America, from Florida and Guale (Georgia) cross-country to the Californias. His volume in the Chronicles of America series staked out this field in 1921. The bulk of his more specialized scholarship deals with selected subjects under this rubric. His name for the field has entered our jargon and is picked up in the Harvard *Guide to American History*.

Bolton's students are myriad—the thousands upon thousands who crowded Wheeler Auditorium, the close to three hundred masters and one hundred doctors, the last most significant to us though not necessarily to Bolton. The roster includes Charles E. Chapman, J. Fred Rippy, Arthur Aiton, Charles W. Hackett, J. Lloyd Mecham, George P. Hammond, Lawrence Hill, John Tate Lanning, Irving Leonard, William Shiels, Peter M. Dunne, Woodrow Borah, John Bannon, and several times that many Latin Americanists. It includes Cardinal Goodwin, William C. Binkley, LeRoy Hafen, Owen C. Coy, the Ellisons, A. P. Nasatir, Lawrence Kinnaird, R. Kay Wyllys, Leland Creer, Wallace Smith, Adele Ogden, Milton Hunter, John Hussey, Philip C. Brooks, John Kemble, Gregory Crampton, and many others more especially concerned with the American West. These students were so numerous as to call for two separate *Festschriften—New Spain and the Anglo-American West* in two volumes in 1932, and *Greater America* in 1944. In the latter volume the corpus of the writings of these students took 123 pages to tabulate. It has grown considerably since that date.

Several of these Bolton men turned out

to be reasonably prolific. The most fluent of them, however, face a real challenge to match the poundage and shelfage turned out by their mentor. His voluminous writings are, as we historians take for granted, his chief claim to fame.

The ranks are full of historians whose scholarly bent was forecast by their doctoral dissertations. Not so with Bolton; he did not carry into print his study of the free Negro in the prewar South, nor are any of his later writings traceable to his undergraduate work at Wisconsin or his graduate study at Pennsylvania. At length, however, after two years of teaching at Milwaukee State Teachers College and one at the University of Texas, he found himself intrigued by Texas' Spanish background. In the summer of 1902, he posted off to Mexico to explore the archives and there discovered the materials and the subject that would engage him throughout his career.

Immediately he began to contribute to the *Quarterly* of the Texas State Historical Association. In 1902 appeared a description of some of his manuscript findings; in 1903, a report on Tienda de Cuervo's inspection of Laredo in 1757. For the mammoth collection on the Philippine Islands, edited by Blair and Robertson, he translated eight or ten substantial documents. In 1905, seventy pages in the *Quarterly* were allotted for his monograph-length article on the abandonment and reoccupation of East Texas. Within the course of the next three years, he returned seven more times to the *Quarterly*. Meanwhile, he sent the *American Historical Review* a description of manuscript holdings in Mexico and followed that with a sheaf of papers which the Spaniards had confiscated a hundred years earlier from Zebulon Montgomery Pike.

These publications were not yet a book. They were, nevertheless, substantial, and they had a promising focus on Spanish Texas and its environs. Other criteria, of course, come to bear in faculty recruitment; this was the publication record when Stanford brought Bolton west to a professorship in 1909 and when the University of California lured him a short step northeastward in 1911. At both these institutions there was awareness that Bolton had work in progress that was much more ambitious.

Over the next few years the results began to show. In 1913 his first book appeared, the indestructible *Guide to Materials for the History of the United States in the Principal Archives of Mexico*. In 1914 came his two-volume documentary, *Athanase de Mézières and the Louisiana-Texas Frontier, 1768–1780*. He sent another half-dozen contributions to the Texas State Historical Association's now rechristened *Southwestern Historical Quarterly*, and in 1915 brought this material into a roundup volume, *Texas in the Middle Eighteenth Century*. A plump sourcebook, *Spanish Exploration in the Southwest, 1542–1706*, followed the next year.

In this decade evidence mounted that Bolton's horizons were broadening to other Spanish frontiers. In addition to what he had found on Pike, he had manuscript discoveries to report on California's Portolá and on the

"Lost History" by Pimería's Kino. He translated a Pedro Fages diary recounting the first return visit to San Francisco Bay, in 1770. He commented on opportunities for research in Nevada history and California history. He published a note on Spanish fur trade on the Missouri and a longer paper on French intrusions into New Mexico, 1749–52. And, in 1917, as faculty research lecturer—a high honor bestowed by his peers at Berkeley—he was ready to generalize on "The Mission as a Frontier Institution in the Spanish Colonies." Two years later appeared another two-volume documentary, *Kino's Historical Memoir of Pimería Alta.*

The twenties saw the publication of his two major syntheses, *The Colonization of North America* (with T. M. Marshall), and *The Spanish Borderlands.* In 1925 came the Georgia harvest: *Arredondo's Historical Proof of Spain's Title to Georgia* and (with Mary Ross) *The Debatable Land.* Following a stimulating paper on "The Mormons in the Opening of the West," the pendulum swung to California for ten volumes of documents,

Palóu's *Historical Memoirs of New California; Fray Juan Crespi, Missionary Explorer;* and *Anza's California Expeditions.*

Ushering in the thirties, he did a series of historical vignettes for *Touring Topics,* predecessor of *Westways* as the organ of the Automobile Club of Southern California. These were subsequently reissued as *Cross, Sword, and Gold Pan.* In 1932, as his presidential address to the American Historical Association, "The Epic of Greater America," he presented the case for the hemispheric perspective. To his favorite frontiersman, Eusebio Francisco Kino, he paid loving tribute, first in a sketch, *The Padre on Horseback,* in 1932, and then in full-scale biography, *Rim of Christendom,* in 1936.

In 1937, with spontaneity and élan he welcomed the discovery of Drake's Plate of Brass. Two years later, under the title *Wider Horizons of American History,* he brought together four papers in which his featured themes stood forth. First came "The Epic of Greater America," buttressed by "Defensive Spanish Expansion and the Significance of the Borderlands." Then followed "The Mission as a Frontier Institution in the Spanish Colonies," supported in somewhat narrower focus by "The Black Robes of New Spain."

Two major works were yet to come: *Coronado on the Turquoise Trail* (1949) and *Pageant in the Wilderness: The Story of the Escalante Expedition to the Interior Basin* (1950).

Bolton's writings can be divided into three parts. He published aids to scholarship and to teaching—his syllabus on *The History of the Americas,* first as a paperback and then in a clothbound edition in 1928; his series of maps; his numerous notes and articles descriptive of archival holdings; and the *Guide* to United States history material in the Mexican archives. This *Guide,* vintage 1913, is still the best finding tool in its field. At the Bancroft Library, ask for the Bible and this is what they will bring out.

Bolton devoted many of his busy years to translating and editing original documents. This part of his work began with contributions to the Blair and Robertson set on the

Philippine Islands and advanced to the volumes or sets of volumes on De Mézières, Kino, Arredondo, Paloú, Crespi, Anza, and Escalante. Critics have said that, having demonstrated his capacity at this allegedly menial chore, a great historian should have moved on to more creative scholarship. Yet Bolton had a special flair as a translator. He entered into each piece of writing as though it were his own. In the introduction and notes to these volumes he found opportunity to be creative. Is there any one of these translations that we wish he had not done?

His monographs and biographies are another stout shelf. His biography of Kino, *Rim of Christendom* (1936), deserves consideration as his most impressive work, though how to compare such a book with the five volumes of *Anza's California Expeditions* (1930) is not clearly revealed.

Works of wide scope come down to two: *The Colonization of North America* (1920) and *The Spanish Borderlands* (1921). Bolton fully intended to add to them a broad canvas on the history of the Americas. He talked about it constantly and to such an extent that he pre-empted the field without publishing the book. Why he did not carry through is something I cannot fully explain. I cannot perform a diagnosis in the manner that Ray Billington did of Frederick Jackson Turner.

I am sure Bolton did not want this book to have the pedestrian quality of the *Colonization* volume. He wanted it to be rich in detail, a major strength in his *Outpost of Empire* and *Rim of Christendom*. It was one thing, however, to get that kind of verve in books of small compass, and something else to achieve it in a work with continental sweep. In chapter drafts that he read to me, his enthusiasm for the narrative seemed likely to carry him to a ten-volume work rather than a more practical two. I can imagine other deterrents. After awhile, the all-knowing bookmen were saying that the course was going into decline and that it was too late for such a book. Bolton did not bring out his history of the hemisphere.

Although almost half of his graduate

students became Western Americanists, Bolton is almost always classified as a Latin Americanist. It is true that under his direction the Bancroft Library turned its major efforts to acquisitions on Spanish North America—the southern third or quarter of what had been Hubert Howe Bancroft's search list. Since Bolton was both a Latin Americanist and a western history man, what has led so many astray may have been his own inspiration in naming his favorite field the Spanish borderlands. Had he called it the "American borderlands once Spanish," there might be more recognition that the great bulk of his writing is pertinent to the history of the American West.

It can be argued that his idea of the continental or hemispheric perspective is the most advisable setting for studies that may seem to be contained within the United States, including studies of the American West. Also it can be argued that his Spanish borderlands belong as an ingredient in the histories both of Spanish America and of the United States or the American West.

Since Bolton concentrated on colonial studies—America's ancient history—it was inevitable that, as time went on, his subject matter and his findings would seem to have less bearing on the present and its problems.

His dream for hemisphere history has not come true.

His borderlands history struck many historians as "way out"—a fringe area to Spanish America, and a fringe area to the United States and thus to the American West. If that were so, there would be fewer historians eligible to listen to him than to Frederick Jackson Turner, who generalized on the whole West and, in fact, on the whole nation, or to Walter Prescott Webb, who generalized on the whole world. His Spanish borderlands are rejected by Latin Americanists and neglected by historians of the West. The general histories and bibliographies of Latin America often are constructed as though these outlying provinces were never Spanish. Western writers tend to treat them as though they were an exotic prior figuration extraneous to all that developed later.

## Herbert Eugene Bolton

Bolton's ideas may have been rebuffed, but his writings have not been supplanted, and there is no reason to think that they will soon be in need of redoing. His students and his students' students are a sizable work force, and their writings constitute a significant supplement to his own. A good fraction bear on the American West.

For the foreseeable future he has prodigious stature. He was the foremost trainer of Latin American and Western American scholars and, by the statistics, a worthy successor to Hubert Howe Bancroft. He is ripe for legend as the Paul Bunyan of western historians.

# Selected Bibliography

## HERBERT EUGENE BOLTON

---

## BOOKS

*The Philippine Islands, 1493–1803.* E. H. Blair and J. A. Robertson, eds. 55 vols. Translations of documents in volumes V, VI, XVIII, and XIX. Cleveland, 1903–09.

*Guide to Materials for the History of the United States in the Principal Archives of Mexico.* Washington, D.C.: Carnegie Institute, 1913.

*Athanase de Mézières and the Louisiana-Texas Frontier, 1768–1780.* 2 vols. Cleveland: Clark, 1914.

*Texas in the Middle Eighteenth Century: Studies in Spanish Colonial History and Administration.* Berkeley: University of California Press, 1915.

*Spanish Exploration in the Southwest, 1542–1706.* New York: Charles Scribner's Sons, 1916; 1930.

"The Early Explorations of Father Garcés on the

Pacific Slope," with H. M. Stephens, in *The Pacific Ocean in History*. New York: Macmillan, 1917. Pp. 317–30.

*Kino's Historical Memoir of Pimería Alta*. 2 vols. Cleveland: Clark, 1919.

*The Colonization of North America*, with T. M. Marshall. New York: Macmillan, 1920.

*The Spanish Borderlands*. New Haven: Yale University Press, 1921.

*California's Story*, with E. D. Adams. Boston, 1922.

*Arredondo's Historical Proof of Spain's Title to Georgia*. Berkeley: University of California Press, 1925.

*The Debatable Land: A Sketch of the Anglo-Spanish Contest for the Georgia Country*, with Mary Ross. Berkeley: University of California Press, 1925.

*Historical Memoirs of New California, by Fray Francisco Palóu*. 4 vols. Berkeley: University of California Press, 1926.

*Fray Juan Crespi, Missionary Explorer on the Pacific Coast*. Berkeley: University of California Press, 1927.

*History of the Americas: A Syllabus with Maps*. Boston: Ginn & Co., 1928; 1935.

*Anza's California Expeditions*. 5 vols. Berkeley: University of California Press, 1930; Vol. I reissued as *Outpost of Empire*. New York: Knopf, 1931; Vol. IV reissued as *Font's Complete Diary*. Berkeley: University of California Press, 1931.

*The Padre on Horseback*. San Francisco: Sonora

Press, 1932; Chicago: Loyola University Press, 1963.

*Cross, Sword, and Gold Pan.* Los Angeles, 1936.

*Rim of Christendom: A Biography of Eusebio Francisco Kino, Pacific Coast Pioneer.* New York: Macmillan, 1936.

*Wider Horizons of American History.* New York: D. Appleton-Century, 1939.

*Coronado on the Turquoise Trail, Knight of Pueblos and Plains.* Albuquerque: University of New Mexico Press, 1949.

*Pageant in the Wilderness: The Story of the Escalante Expedition to the Interior Basin, 1776.* Salt Lake City, 1950.

## PERIODICALS

"Some Materials for Southwestern History in the Archivo General de México," Texas State Historical Association *Quarterly*, VI (1902), 103–12; VII (1904), 196–213.

"Tienda de Cuervo's Ynspección de Laredo, 1757," TSHAQ, VI (1903), 187–203.

"The Spanish Abandonment and Re-occupation of East Texas, 1773–1779," TSHAQ, IX (1905), 67–137.

"The Founding of Mission Rosario," TSHAQ, X (1907), 113–39.

"Spanish Mission Records at San Antonio," TSHAQ, X (1907), 297–307.

"Material for Southwestern History in the Central

Archives of Mexico," *American Historical Review,* XIII (1908), 510–27.

"The Native Tribes about the East Texas Missions," TSHAQ, XI (1908), 249–76.

"Notes on Clark's 'The Beginnings of Texas,'" TSHAQ, XII (1908), 148–58.

"Papers of Zebulon M. Pike, 1806–1807," *AHR,* XIII (1908), 798–827.

"Expedition to San Francisco Bay in 1770: Diary of Pedro Fages," Academy of Pacific Coast History, *Publications,* II (1911), 141–59.

"Father Kino's Lost History, Its Discovery and Its Value," Bibliographical Society of America, *Papers,* VI (1911), 9–34.

"The Jumano Indians in Texas, 1650–1771," TSHAQ, XV (1911), 66–84.

"The Obligation of Nevada toward the Writing of Her Own History," Nevada Historical Society, *Report* (1913), 62–79.

"The Spanish Occupation of Texas, 1519–1690," *Southwestern Historical Quarterly,* XVI (1912), 1–26.

"The Admission of California," University of California *Chronicle,* XV (1913), 554–66.

"Spanish Activities on the Lower Trinity River, 1746–1771," *SHQ,* XVI (1913), 339–77.

"New Light on Manuel Lisa and the Spanish Fur Trade," *SHQ,* XVII (1913), 61–66.

"The Founding of the Missions on the San Gabriel River, 1745–1749," *SHQ,* XVII (1914), 323–78.

# John W. Caughey

"The Location of La Salle's Colony on the Gulf of Mexico," *Mississippi Valley Historical Review,* II (1915), 165–82.

"French Intrusions into New Mexico, 1749–1752," *ibid.,* 389–407.

"The Mission as a Frontier Institution in the Spanish-American Colonies," *AHR,* XXIII (1917), 42–61.

"General James Wilkinson as Advisor to Emperor Iturbide," *Hispanic American Historical Review,* I (1918), 163–80.

"Father Escobar's Relation of the Oñate Expedition to California," *Catholic Historical Review,* V (1919), 19–41.

"The Iturbide Revolution in the Californias," *HAHR,* II (1919), 188–242.

"The Mormons in the Opening of the West," *Utah Genealogical and Historical Magazine,* XVI (1926), 40–72.

"Escalante in Dixie and the Arizona Strip," *New Mexico Historical Review,* III (1928), 41–72.

"Defensive Spanish Expansion and the Significance of the Borderlands," in *The Trans-Mississippi West* (Boulder, 1930), 1–42.

"In the South San Joaquín ahead of Garcés," *California Historical Society Quarterly,* X (1931), 211–19.

"The Epic of Greater America," *AHR,* XXXVIII (1933), 448–74.

"The Black Robes of New Spain," *Catholic Historical Review,* XXI (1935), 257–82.

## Herbert Eugene Bolton

"The Jesuits in America: An Opportunity for Historians," *Mid-America*, XVIII (1936), 223–33.

"Francis Drake's Plate of Brass," *Drake's Plate of Brass*. San Francisco, 1937. Pp. 1–16.

### WRITINGS ABOUT BOLTON

John Francis Bannon, ed. *Bolton and the Spanish Borderlands*. Norman: University of Oklahoma Press, 1964.

Frederick E. Bolton. "The Early Life of Herbert E. Bolton: From Random Memories of an Admiring Brother," *Arizona and the West*, IV (1962), 65–73.

Caughey, John W. "Herbert Eugene Bolton," *Pacific Historical Review*, XXII (1953), 109–12.

Hammond, George P., ed. *New Spain and the Anglo-American West: Historical Contributions Presented to Herbert Eugene Bolton*. 2 vols. [Los Angeles], 1932.

Hanke, Lewis, ed. *Do the Americas Have a Common History? A Critique of the Bolton Theory*. New York: Alfred A. Knopf, 1964.

Adele Ogden, ed. *Greater America: Essays in Honor of Herbert Eugene Bolton*. Berkeley: University of California Press, 1945.

Walter Prescott Webb, 1954

*Joe B. Frantz*

# WALTER PRESCOTT WEBB

I N THE periodic western trinity of Herbert Eugene Bolton, Frederick Jackson Turner, and Walter Prescott Webb, it is mildly curious that only one of these justifiably famous historians was what we envious tradesmen designate as a producer. With almost Presbyterian devotion, Turner researched for signs from heaven above and earth below confirming or disavowing the sanctity of his presumption, while Bolton billygoated down *barrancas* and marched across *malpais,* always with enough energy left over to go home and

[75]

write, as Texas artist Buck Schiwetz would say, with a venom.

In this area Webb stands somewhere in between. He clambered across the country-side, returning home not so much to research as to put his feet on his desk, look out the window and dream, and just now and then write like a man possessed. But no steady stream of books and articles emanated from his Texas typewriter, because he liked to look and think and talk and know what he was going to say before he committed himself to paper. And when he did write, he never thought of himself as a western historian, but as a universally minded writer whose universe just happened to come home to the American West with some frequency.

Like any good teacher or writer, he enjoyed explaining to someone who might know less about a subject than he. And no matter what he wrote about, he always wrote primarily for one person—not the specter of a critical book-reviewer, as most historians do, but an imaginary Bostonian who was not a professional historian, writer, or critic but a man of wide culture who could feel at home at Locke-Ober's, Fenway Park, or even the Old Howard, and who could be interested in a slice of non-Bostonian history. To an inestimable degree, much of the clarity which came to characterize Webb's prose resulted from his asking himself, as he read back over his copy, whether he had made his Bostonian understand what he was trying to say. As for historians, Webb largely felt that they read little except what was practical in pursuit of their research problems, and he refused to write for them, either in general or in the particular.

Webb represents that class of historian-writers who, to the horror of dedicated graduate students, gained fame doing something other than they had intended. (Maybe it was something in the formidable Texas climate, for Bolton also became an academic turncoat while in Texas.) Originally Webb wanted to be a writer, to use words to escape the arid environment in which he was reared. Deliberately he set out to be what he was not; adjectives like "urbane," "cosmopolitan," and "worldly-wise" attracted him, and he tried writing fiction that bordered on the drawing-room genre. But the first articles he sold, and subsequently the first and only fiction, had western themes, for he quickly learned that he could write best as a thinking reporter, a man who examines and portrays perceptively things he knows something about. Distrusting his imagination, he became a historian-teacher, banking on the unexciting surety of a school payroll to keep him solvent and leaning on the everlasting arms of historical fact to keep him "safe and secure from all alarms."

But Webb could no more avoid being a writer than the old-time Fundamentalist preacher could fight the call. And so, as his confidence and practice grew, he became less the traditional historian and more the writer-artist. As he developed as an artist, he broadened his perceptions even as he perfected his technique, so that in the latter years he ranged well beyond the West, drawing his prose pictures from a variety of sources, both historical and topical. And he also became what

How the Republican Party lost Its future.

~~Why the Republican Party Has Failed~~

By Walter Prescott Webb

Senator Henry Cabot Lodge, Jr., published an article in
the Saturday Evening Post of January 29,1949, entitled "Does the
Republican Party Have A Future?" Though he spoke with objectivity,
the fact that he could ask the question indicates that he realizes
the dilemma ~~serious plight~~ of the party of which he is a distinguished
member.   It is probably the first time in the history of the
party that the question was asked in such seriousness.  Senator
Lodge believes the party has a future, but he suggests ~~acknowledges~~ that
it can be realized only on condition that it cleans house, discards
old concepts, and adopts a program more in ~~in greater~~ conformity ~~to~~ with
the will and the aspirations of the American people.   In short
he ~~Senator Lodge~~ implies that the house is in disorder ~~bad order~~, that
its present concepts are archaic and that its program does not
mesh with the spirit and desires ~~aspirations~~ ~~and abilities~~ of the people.

Many thoughtful persons have tried to explain the recent
most surprising defeat of the Republican party, but most of them have
~~been~~ been content to do so it by analyzing the current situation,
in terms of such factors as the labor vote, the farm vote, or
the Roosevelt vote.  ~~Not with standing these attempts~~ At least
I have read no present state of the Republican party
account that has ~~has~~ viewed the problem down the long gunbarrel
of history.   I believe that history throws a strong ~~light~~ clear
a once very powerful
light on the problem and makes  the eclipse of ~~the Republican~~
institution
~~party~~ understandable.

he could not achieve in the 1920's—urbane, cosmopolitan, and worldly-wise, with just enough of the earth showing through to season his speech and titillate his readers.

Always, though, he wanted to be the artist, and nothing is more revealing than when at the close of the great depression, Fred Shannon attacked his *Great Plains,* contending, among other things, that it was not good history. Webb replied—the only time he ever replied to a critic—that he did not think of the book as history but as art. And any intelligent person knows that art is not confined to the narrow precepts and practices of history.

On the other hand, Webb did not downgrade history as a discipline or a profession. Once when I remarked casually that since history was a branch of literature, I therefore wished that historians would pay more attention to the craft of literature, he stopped me short: "Oh, no," he said, "you're backwards. Literature is a branch of history, as is all knowledge."

Webb, who loved such sweeping generalities, never paused to qualify. He was guilty of oversimplification, but again, simplification as he practiced it was a part of the art of communicating in a world of historians, not to mention other breeds, who could not speak more complexly if they set out to confuse. As an example, he told the students at the University of Mississippi that they could handle the racial question by simply getting rich and letting the Negro get rich alongside them— and he almost got run out of the state for his solution.

He told a class at Texas: "I have never known Nature to make an unpleasant sound." And we could take exception to that.

Periodically Webb would complain, like any good son, that his father, who must have had a mind much like his but a disposition considerably more contentious, never appreciated his success. "My father only respected doctors and lawyers," he would say.

Actually Webb's father had more grounds for appreciation than he realized, because aside from the artistry involved, Webb approached a historical problem much like a lawyer, an advocate, preparing a brief. He already had his judge or jury foreman in mind—that would be the mythical Bostonian. Knowing the verdict he wanted, Webb set out to marshal the evidence. In the strict seminar sense, he was a poor researcher, for he had a politician's gift for ignoring contrary evidence. Or, as Frank Dobie said of him, "Webb never lets facts stand in the way of truth."

Like a good lawyer he won more cases—historical cases—than he lost. His book on *The Texas Rangers* is definitive on that frontier enforcement agency, though he came rightly to regard the book as a competent journeyman's job. Later he wrote a "young adolescent's" version which he regarded more highly. "I left out all those deadening facts," he said.

But *The Texas Rangers*, though it has stood up for nearly thirty years, was not an idea book, and therefore never a real favorite with him. Instead, he liked the three for which he is better known—*The Great Plains*, something of a classic; *Divided We Stand*, quickly withdrawn by his publisher because it offended certain corporate directors but quickly republished by Webb himself with the offending chapter intact and never since out of print; and *The Great Frontier,* generally blasted by critics and then forgotten.

In all four of these books Webb acknowledged one overriding influence. As he told the Westerners of Chicago in December, 1959:

In my work in history I have found it impossible to separate a civilization or culture from the physical foundation on which it rests. With this inclination towards physical geography, if that term is not out of date, I was fortunate in choosing the American West as a field of study. I was fortunate because in the American West, the environment is an overwhelming force which has made man and his institutions bend to its imperious influence.

Webb was talking about the geographical and historical concepts essential to an understanding of the American West. The first concept, as he developed it in *The Great Plains* in 1931, "is that of the stark contrast between the East and the West." The ninety-eighth meridian becomes a belt of transition between the humid woodland and the Great Plains with their treelessness, levelness, and semi-aridity. Further, in Webb's view, the ninety-eighth meridian serves as "a sort of institutional fault line separating two physical environments, two animal kingdoms, two vegetable kingdoms, and finally two human cultures, ancient and modern, i.e., Indian and European."

He gives examples. In transportation, eastern rivers are navigable, so that the boat and canoe played important roles in providing cheap and easy transportation. With only three really navigable rivers, the country west of the fault line was essentially without boats, and almost devoid of canoes. Instead, it was the horse that provided transportation in the West.

The West forced a modification of weapons. Because the Indians fought on horseback, the new settlers had to adapt their weapons to mounted warfare. The result, helped along by the Texas Rangers, was the development of the six-shooter. The same thing happened in fences. Whereas the traditional fence east of the ninety-eighth meridian had been made "exclusively of rock or rail, and occasionally with hedges," the pioneer hit a country without rock or rail. Although at first he believed that fencing west of the ninety-eighth meridian was impossible, he shortly turned to the new-fangled barbed wire, bringing orderliness and selectivity to both the dry-land farmer and the owner of the big pasture spread.

A score of other examples could be given, observed Webb, but these three were sufficient. The West just was not like the East, and it had responded by developing its own institutions, sponsored always by differing physical conditions.

Superficially viewed, Webb's next book, *Divided We Stand,* seems almost an aberration from the straight frontier line he supposedly followed. For in this book, published in 1937, he seemed to be pitting two have-not sections of the United States—the West and the South—against an avaricious and wealthy North. Particularly he focused on the economic vassalage of the South, an interest to which he would return with increased optimism in the middle of the 1950's.

Actually *Divided We Stand* lies directly

along the intellectual route from *The Great Plains* to *The Great Frontier.* The subtitle, "The Crisis of a Frontierless Democracy," suggests that something is happening to the frontier, and Webb foresees trouble down the road. "The closing frontier and the growing corporations—both synonymous with decreasing common opportunity—are offered as mated keys to the domestic crisis of the modern world's first great democracy," he writes. The frontier is gone, he opines; left behind are a confused people with no sure place to go.

In *Divided We Stand,* Webb reveals a bit more of himself, especially his fondness for the Democratic party. He states his position backwards: "The most obvious fact is that the South and the West cannot hope to find a solution for their problem through the Republican party as now constituted." The South will continue with the Democrats, he says somewhat mistakenly, "either through ignorance or sentiment or intelligence." On the other hand, the West "has been confused. . . . The West has not always realized that the Republican party is as much a sectional party today as it was during the Civil War, and that western people are not in that section."

To Webb, the South and the West more nearly represented traditional principles of American democracy than the North. But the two sections relied too much on their past and covered their inferiority "by proclaiming that they possess ancient virtues. They emphasize too much for practical purposes their civility or bluster, and yet nothing pleases them so much as to achieve recognition from the North."

After *Divided We Stand*, Webb went into a sort of decline insofar as authorship is concerned. He did have a year as Harkness Lecturer at the University of London, and another year as a wartime Harmsworth Professor at Oxford; but no major publication issued from his aging typewriter. The reason for the silence, aside from the fact that he was buying and selling real estate, establishing a boy's camp called Friday Mountain, fighting individual regents of the University of Texas, and writing transitory pieces, was that he was leading graduate students down a labyrinthine road toward *The Great Frontier.*

The idea for *The Great Frontier,* "of greater magnitude but less originality" than his thesis on the Great Plains (this is Webb's estimate), came to him one spring morning in 1936 when he was working on something entirely unrelated. Two years later he organized a seminar around the idea, and as in *The Great Plains* sent himself and his graduate students questing and digging, this time for fourteen years, until he embalmed the idea in another book.

In his words,

The central question this time was: What effect did the uncovering of three new continents around 1500 have on the civilization that discovered and for a time owned the continents? Again the central question broke up into specific ones. How did the sudden acquisition and subsequent development of all this new land affect the individual? How did it affect such institutions as absolutism, democracy, slavery, and religious polity? Did it do anything to economic practice?

## Walter Prescott Webb

Finding the answers occupied thirteen years of "alternating exaltation and misery" before Webb began to write. But when he did write, he had his theme—the boom hypothesis—and he could write rapidly. The Columbian discoveries of the Great Frontier had precipitated a boom on the European metropolis, giving birth to such new institutions as modern democracy, capitalism, and the idea of progress. This "big boom, based on all the resources of the Great Frontier, lasted so long that it was considered normal and its institutions permanent."

But the boom began to play out as the Great Frontier, of which the American frontier was but a fragment, closed down. The closing brought strains to democracy and capitalism and wounded seriously the idea of progress. Since then, according to Webb, the Western world has been fighting a defensive action as it tries either to restore the boom or develop new institutions and ideas. Historians of future centuries, said Webb, may well look back on the period from 1500 to

1950 as "the most abnormal period in the history of mankind."

As already noted, critics worked over *The Great Frontier* rather thoroughly. Although Clifton Fadiman wrote that it was his nominee for the Pulitzer Prize, most reviewers seized upon its details, if not its general thesis, to point out the inadequacies of Webb's thinking. As for the general reading public, the thesis left little hope for recapturing the exhilaration as well as the wistfulness of a four-hundred-year boom period. Basically it ended on a gloomy note, and the 1950's was not a period for that sort of gloom-spreading. There were even demands, not serious, for Webb's dismissal from the University of Texas. Webb had promised himself the fastest, jazziest Oldsmobile on the market if *The Great Frontier* sold forty thousand copies. He continued to drive Plymouths.

Nonetheless, when Webb died on March 8, 1963, he believed that *The Great Frontier* was his most enduring book. Again, to resume the art analogy of which he was so fond, like any garret-starving painter, Webb was confident and almost content that the thinking public along about 1990 would acclaim his boom hypothesis. Just as *The Great Plains* had known its valleys before it was acclaimed from the American historical mountaintop, *The Great Frontier*, with its international implications, would rise a generation later.

And Webb witnessed just enough success to be encouraged. He was invited to an international meeting in Paris to explain his idea, while in 1958 the Second International Congress of Historians of the United States and Mexico enlarged its attendance to include frontier historians from Australia, Argentina, Brazil, England, Canada, Spain, and France, who spent parts of three days buttressing and excising portions of the Great Frontier idea. Webb felt that men like Sir Keith Hancock, Daniel Cosío-Villegas, and Geoffrey Barraclough would not waste three days on material that was entirely synthetic or superficial.

Actually Webb wrote or edited a great deal more than these four books. More than a score of books, in fact. Little books—half-history, half-propaganda, like *More Water for Texas;* collector's items, like *Flat Top: A Story of Modern Ranching;* several text-books at the elementary and high school levels; a style book for Dun & Bradstreet reporters; the indispensable tool of all writers on the Texas scene, the 953-page, two-volume *Handbook of Texas;* or the happy editing of the 1963 best-seller, *Washington Wife.*

In between he wrote numerous magazine articles. The greatest controversy was stirred by his May, 1957, article in *Harper's,* in which he pointed out that the unifying force of the American West was its desert qualities. The idea of the Great American Desert was not new, having been part of the literature and cartography of nineteenth-century ex-plorations. But as people had settled and areas had become organized, the desert idea had been dispelled as a sort of subversive igno-rance proclaimed from the Atlantic side of the Mississippi. The word "desert" has unpleas-ant connotations.

But as Webb told the Chicago Westerners,

"the desert did not know it had been abolished, and so it sat quiet as deserts do, and grimly determined not only the pattern of settlement but the mode of life of its would-be conquerors." The story of the West then, in Webb's mind, is a story of deficiencies—in water, trees, cities, industry, organized labor, Negroes, and history. Its wealth lay in its rim areas, nearly all of which are in turn running out of water.

A storm of vituperation and outrage ensued. Webb was told that if he didn't like the West, he should go back from whence he came. The Denver *Post* warned him to "pull off your glasses and lay down your Ph.D. because you have picked yourself a fight." The Phoenix *Gazette* entitled its editorial "An Insult to Arizona and the West," while Senator Gordon Allott of Colorado suggested that Webb ought to travel the West and get acquainted with it. One woman wanted to come to Austin to spit on Webb's building, while another writer was ready to use him as target practice.

Webb's reaction fluctuated between delight

and dismay. He was delighted to have stirred up so much interest in the West, but dismayed that he might have ridden his idea overhard. But the experts in the United States Department of Agriculture, in western universities, and in the scientific and literary world backed him up almost completely. He did take seriously those letters which criticized him soberly, and tried to answer them with care and sensitivity. As he wrote one disturbed Nevadan:

I could write quite an essay on the character of the people of the West, their courage, their friendliness, their integrity. They make up for many of the shortcomings of the land. They have the adventurous spirit, have to have it. If I have forfeited their friendship, it is a matter of deep regret. My purpose was to help them understand their country and themselves.

Meanwhile Webb was becoming increasingly redirected toward the South. In early 1963 he officially resigned as the prospective author of a volume on the American West for the New American Nation series to get to work trying to convince the South that the next century belonged to it as the great under-exploited section of the nation if it wouldn't get inextricably snarled in its racial tangle. "I want the son of a bitch to know what it it feels like to be rich," he told one Southern audience to whom he carried his latest gospel.

On the other hand, Webb and I had accepted advances to turn out one of these overpriced picture books on the West—he to do the text while I gathered the art work. To prepare himself in an area in which he felt a lack of knowledge, he had taught the summer of 1962 at the University of Alaska, suffering the pangs of a two-months' separation from his bride of six months and acknowledging with his frequent sour grin, "I prefer the frontier in theory over the frontier in fact."

Webb loved to fool with piecework, perhaps to the detriment of more solid accomplishments but all adding to his understanding. Thus he wrote drafts of speeches for national and local politicians; he served a tour as an idea man for then Senator Lyndon B. Johnson; he was always available for a guest column for a newspaper. He wrote introductions by the barrelful—to a book of Texas art, about which he knew little; to a history of Masonry, of which he knew less. Typical of his method—or lack of method—is the just-mentioned article he wrote for *Harper's* on the West as a desert culture. He had read something or other by Lucius Beebe which he thought as spurious as all get-out, and he wrote a review of the book for the Dallas *News*. But with a desk that invariably resembled a surrealist's nightmare, he lost the review before he could get it in the mail. Annoyed at having to rewrite, he checked up on his facts; one led to another, and the first thing he knew he had a full-length article, too long for a book page. Since he always preferred articulate popular magazines to the professional journals—he actually published little except presidential addresses in the reviews—he sent the article to *Harper's*, which made sure that every vocal chamber of commerce and sensitive governor in the West saw a copy.

Webb's personal background may account to some extent for his wavering between extreme isolation and complete involvement in controversy. Reared in an impoverished West Texas area by parents who were "destitute products of the Civil War," he grew up with little formal schooling but with an unswerving determination to escape the bleakness of a wind-swept farm. Through a chance subscription to *The Sunny South*, he was encouraged to write a letter to that journal which appeared in its May 14, 1904, issue. It was a simple letter, as straightforward and brief as an honest, teen-age, undereducated farm boy might be expected to write. In it, Webb said he wanted to be a writer and to get an education, and could someone tell him how.

Out of nowhere—Brooklyn actually—came a reply from a bachelor importer of novelties, William E. Hinds. Hinds told the youth to "keep your mind fixed on a lofty purpose and your hopes will be realized. . . . I will be glad to send you some books or magazines." A windfall of books and magazines began to come to the print-starved boy, firing his imagination and also firing "to white heat my desire for an education." His craving for something beyond the rural life reached through to his father, who promised the youth voluntarily that if they made a good crop, he would move the family into the little town of Ranger, so that Walter could go to school for one year and perhaps pass the examination for a teacher's certificate.

When the year 1905 turned out to be a good crop year, with the rains coming on schedule in that often-parched land, Casner Webb delivered on his promise. In turn, the son responded by selling his "trim blue mare, close-built, easy to keep, fast, and lovely to look at" for $60.00 for school books, sweeping the school for tuition, and feeding the suction pipe at the Ranger cotton gin to help with family expenses. The gamble paid off when the following summer he received a second-grade certificate permitting him to teach in rural schools.

That first year after "graduation" Webb taught three schools—one for six weeks, one for four months, and one for two months at salaries from $42.50 to $45.00 a month. He saved his money, went to school another year, and received a first-grade certificate, followed by a new appointment at $75.00 a month, the maximum salary in the county.

And then one cold January day in 1909, "so windy that the pebbles from the playing field rattled like buckshot against the side of the school building," Webb heard from Hinds. In part the letter read as follows:

. . . the best thing in life is to help some one, if we can. One would count it a great thing (to remember) if they had helped someone, that had afterwards become famous or great, say for instance Lincoln or Gladstone. . . . And perhaps I can say, "Why I helped J. Prescott Webb* when he was a young man." And people may look at me, as a privileged character to have had the opportunity; so my boy tell me about your plans and hopes and then perhaps I may be able to help you carry them out.

If Hinds had lived fifteen years longer, he still would have received little return on his investment. In fact, it would take almost a third of a century before the gratifications and acknowledgments of fame would begin to make Webb feel that Hinds's faith had been

* For years Hinds mistakenly addressed Webb in this fashion.

[99]

justified. And amid the recognition which
did come, Webb always felt a tincture of regret that Hinds would never know.

How much else do you say about Webb?
How much about his importance in the world
of historians and of ideas? Only this much is
certain right now: his *The Great Plains* influenced men's thinking; the presidential addresses to the Mississippi Valley and American historical associations apparently get
wide attention in seminars devoted to historiography; he wrote several articles that like-
wise have influenced. Beyond that, one can
only conjecture. Will his small book on William E. Hinds, shortly to be published after
arousing considerable attention in *Harper's*
and *Reader's Digest,* turn out to be an inspi-
rational book for the ages? Will *The Great
Frontier* some day be hailed as a book of rare
prophecy, or did Webb ignore too many
fundamentals of world history, sociology, an-
thropology, economics, and political science,
to name only several of the disciples of practitioners who dispraised it? Only our academic children can answer these questions,

when we will be beyond tuning in for the answers.

Certainly we know, too, that the facts of Webb's belated arrival on the academic scene have given pause to many a graduate history faculty, not alone at Chicago and Texas. I don't know how many times Webb grunted to us younger members of the Texas department who were being critical of a prospective new employee because at nineteen he still lacked a year on his Ph.D., had only five articles to his credit, and no books.

"You fellows," he was wont to say, "never *would* have hired me. If you *had* hired me, you wouldn't have kept me. And if you *had* kept me, you wouldn't have promoted me. I came along at the latest possible moment to have made good in this profession. But since the University didn't push me, I have tried in my way to show my appreciation of its patience."

Perhaps the largest significance of Webb's career may ultimately lie in the fact that in a profession dedicated to demonstrable activity, Webb's career acts as a flashing sign that we must still make room along the road for the slower man who takes time to view the scenery and think on what he sees. Certainly he saw, and certainly he thought. And just as certainly Walter Prescott Webb caused men to reassess; whether he was right or wrong hardly seems important—what matters is that he forced men to look anew at a part of the story of how we came to be where we are, and what we are.

To Webb, looking afresh was education. Like Shelley, he believed that teachers do not reap the harvest of the seeds they plant because they plant for posterity and mankind. And on at least one occasion he said General William Booth's borrowed quotation should "be written in invisible ink and be framed over the desk" of every teacher and administrator: "Sow the seeds and fear not the birds for the harvest is not yours." Walter Prescott Webb sowed the seeds. The harvest he left to take care of itself.

# Selected Bibliography

## WALTER PRESCOTT WEBB

---

### BOOKS

*Growth of a Nation: The United States of America.* With Eugene C. Barker and William E. Dodd. ("Our Nation History Series.") Evanston, Ill.: Row, Peterson & Co., 1928.

*The Great Plains.* Boston: Ginn & Co., 1931; *Le Grandi Pianure* (Italian edition). Bologna: Societa Editrice il Mulino, 1961.

*The Story of Our Nation: The United States of America.* With Eugene C. Barker and William E. Dodd. ("Our Nation History Series.") Evanston, Ill.: Row, Peterson & Co., 1929.

*Our Nation Begins.* With Eugene C. Barker and William E. Dodd. ("Our Nation History Series.") Evanston, Ill.: Row, Peterson & Co., 1932.

## Joe B. Frantz

*Our Nation Grows Up.* With Eugene C. Barker and William E. Dodd. ("Our Nation History Series.") Evanston, Ill.: Row, Peterson & Co., 1933.

*The Texas Rangers: A Century of a Frontier Defense.* Boston: Houghton Mifflin, 1935.

*The Building of Our Nation.* With Eugene C. Barker and William E. Dodd. ("Our Nation History Series.") Evanston, Ill.: Row, Peterson & Co., 1937.

*Divided We Stand: The Crisis of a Frontierless Democracy.* New York: Farrar & Rinehart, Inc., 1937.

*The Story of Our Country.* With Eugene C. Barker and Marie Alsager. ("Our Nation History Series.") Evanston, Ill.: Row, Peterson & Co., 1941.

*Our New Nation.* With Eugene C. Barker and Frances Cavanah. ("Our Nation History Series.") Evanston, Ill.; Row, Peterson & Co., 1948.

*The Handbook of Texas* (ed.-in-chief). 2 vols. Texas Historical Association, 1950.

*The Great Frontier.* Boston: Houghton Mifflin, 1952.

*More Water for Texas: The Problem and the Plan.* Austin: University of Texas Press, 1954.

*Our New Land.* With Eugene C. Barker and Frances Cavanah. ("Our Nation History Series.") Evanston, Ill.: Row, Peterson & Co., 1955.

*The Story of the Texas Rangers.* New York: Grosset & Dunlap, 1957.

*An Honest Preface and Other Essays.* Boston: Houghton Mifflin, 1959.

*Flat Top: A Story of Modern Ranching.* El Paso: Carl Hertzog, 1960.

# Walter Prescott Webb

*Washington Wife: From the Journal of Ellen Maury Slayden* (ed.). New York: Harper & Row, 1963.

## PAPERS, ADDRESSES, ARTICLES
## BY WEBB IN PERIODICALS AND BOOKS

"The Texas Rangers in the Mexican War." Unpublished master's thesis, Department of History, University of Texas, 1920.

"The Last Treaty of the Republic of Texas," *Southwestern Historical Quarterly*, Vol. 25, No. 3 (January, 1922).

"The Thirteenth Notch" (fiction), *Frontier*, 1924.

"The American Revolver and the West," *Scribner's Magazine*, Vol. LXXXI, No. 2 (February, 1927).

"The Great Plains and the Industrial Revolution," in *The Trans-Mississippi West*, eds. James F. Willard and Colin B. Goodykoontz. Boulder: University of Colorado Press, 1929.

"The Singing Snakes of the Karankawas," *Southwest Review*, Vol. XXII, No. 4 (July, 1937); also in *Southwestern Writers*, eds. T. M. Pearce and A. P. Thomason. Albuquerque: University of New Mexico Press, 1946.

"Texas: Eternal Triangle of the Southwest," *Saturday Review of Literature*, Vol. XXV, No. 20 (May 16, 1942).

"They Rode Straight Up to Death," in *Roundup Time*, ed. George Sessions Perry. New York: McGraw-Hill Book Co., 1943.

"Cultural Resources of Texas," in *Texas Looks Ahead*, ed. Lorena Drummond (*The Resources of Texas,* Vol. I). Austin: University of Texas Press, 1944.

"Life in an English University," *Southwest Review,* Vol. XXIX, No. 3 (Spring, 1944).

"How the Republican Party Lost Its Future," *Southwest Review,* Vol. XXXVII, No. 4 (Autumn, 1949).

"The Ranger Runs Down a Rumor," *The Ranger,* Vol. 62, No. 6 (March, 1950).

"Ended: Four Hundred Year Boom," *Harper's Magazine,* Vol. CCIII, No. 1217 (October, 1951); also in *A Quarto of Modern Literature,* eds. Leonard Brown and Porter G. Perrin. New York: Charles Scribner's Sons, 1957.

"Windfalls of the Frontier," *Harper's Magazine,* Vol. CCIII, No. 1218 (November, 1951).

"Dynamics of Property in the Modern World," *Southwest Review,* Vol. XXXVII, No. 4 (Autumn, 1952).

"The Great Frontier and Modern Literature," *Southwest Review,* Vol. XXVII, No. 2 (Spring, 1952).

"Points of View: An Honest Preface," *Southwest Review,* Vol. XXVII, No. 2 (Spring, 1952).

"Billion Dollar Cure for Texas Drought," *Harper's Magazine,* Vol. CCVII, No. 1243 (December, 1953).

"The Age of the Frontier," in *Perspectives USA,* No. 11 (Spring, 1955).

"The Historical Seminar: Its Outer Shell and Its Inner Spirit," *Mississippi Valley Historical Review,* Vol. XLII, No. 1 (June, 1955).

## Walter Prescott Webb

"The Frontier and the 400 Year Boom," in *The Turner Thesis Concerning the Role of the Frontier in American History*, ed. George Rogers Taylor (rev. ed.). Boston: D. C. Heath & Co., 1956.

"The American West, Perpetual Mirage," *Harper's Magazine*, Vol. CCXIV (May, 1957).

"The Desert Is Its Heart," *Saturday Review*, Vol. 40 (December 28, 1957).

"The Western World Frontier," in *The Frontier in Perspective*, eds. Walker D. Wyman and Clifton B. Kroeber. Madison: University of Wisconsin Press, 1957.

"The West and the Desert," in *Montana, The Magazine of Western History*, Vol. 8, No. 1 (January, 1958).

"The South and the Golden Slippers," *The Texas Quarterly*, Vol. I, No. 2 (Spring, 1958).

"The Cattle Kingdom," in *The Cowboy Reader*, eds. Lon Tinkle and Allen Maxwell. New York: Longmans, Green & Co., 1959.

"History as High Adventure," *American Historical Review*, Vol. LXIX, No. 2 (January, 1959); also in *The Texas Quarterly*, Vol. II, No. 2 (Summer, 1959).

"The South's Call to Greatness: Challenge to All Southerners," *Texas Business Review*, Vol. 33, No. 10 (October, 1959).

"The South's Economic Prospect," address, in *The Industrialization of the South*. Princeton, N.J.: Princeton University Press, 1960.

"My Search for William E. Hinds," *Harper's Magazine*, Vol. CCXXIII (July, 1961).

"Washington Wife: From the Journal of Ellen Maury Slayden" (ed.), *Southwest Review*, XLVIII, No. 1 (Winter, 1963).

## CRITICISM OF WEBB'S WRITINGS

Shannon, Fred A. *An Appraisal of the Great Plains: A Study in Institutions and Environment*, by Walter Prescott Webb. New York: Social Science Research Council, 1940.

Caughey, John W. "A Criticism of the Critique of Webb's 'The Great Plains,'" *Mississippi Valley Historical Review*, Vol. XXVIII, No. 3 (December, 1940).

Fleming, Roscoe. "Frontier-Style Historian," *Christian Science Monitor* (April 16, 1963).

Parker, Franklin. "Walter Prescott Webb, 1888–1963: Western Historian," *Journal of the West* (July, 1963).

Rundell, Walter, Jr. "Walter Prescott Webb: Product of Environment," *Arizona and the West* (Spring, 1963).

*The Texas Observer*, Austin, Texas, Vol. 55, No. 17 (July 26, 1963). A special issue devoted entirely to Dr. Webb, containing articles by J. Frank Dobie, Wilson Hudson, Joe B. Frantz, and others.

Frantz, Joe B. "Walter Prescott Webb," *The American West*, Vol. I, No. 1 (Winter, 1964).

# INDEX

Adams, Henry: Turner on, 12
Allen, William F., 27
Allott, Gordon (senator), 93
American Historical Association: Bolton as president, 51, 55. *See also* "The Epic of Greater America"
*American Historical Review,* 58
American West: Turner's concept of western development, 6, 8–10; Turner's definition of frontier and West, 7–10, 13–15; Turner on, 31; Bolton develops students of, 55–56, 64–65; and Bolton's hemispheric approach to history, 53, 54–55, 65–67; and Bolton's theory of Spanish borderlands, 55, 65–66; Bolton influences historiography of, 66–67; Webb as writer of, 76–77;

Webb on, 83–84, 92–93; Webb contrasts West and East, 84–85; similarity to South, 86–87. *See also* Boom hypothesis, Desert, Frontier process, "Genetic element," Great Plains, History, Spanish borderlands
*Arizona and the West,* 43
"Aspects of the Westward Movement in American History," 6–8

Bancroft, Hubert Howe, 65–67
Bancroft Library: Bolton as director, 41, 46, 65; mentioned, 62
Barraclough, Geoffrey, 91
Beard, Charles A.: on Turner's ideas, 15, 33
Becker, Carl: Turner corresponds with, 14, 17, 24–

[109]

# Index

# Index

# Index

American West, Biography, Boom hypothesis, Conclusions, Frontier process, "Genetic element," Science

Huntington Library, 3n, 6, 10n

Johnson, Lyndon B. (senator), 95

Kino, Eusebio Francisco, 59, 61, 62, 63

McCormac, Eugene I., 48
Marshall, T. M., 53
Merk, Frederick, 8
Mexico: Bolton's research in archives, 53, 55, 57–59; mentioned, *passim*
"The Mission as a Frontier Institution in the Spanish Colonies," 62
Mood, Fulmer: on Turner, 25
"The Mormons in the Opening of the West," 61

*New Spain and the Anglo-American West,* 56
Newspapers: reaction to Webb article, 93

Paetow, Louis, 48
Parkman, Francis: contrasted with Turner, 3
Perspective, historical: *see* Historical perspective
Philippine Islands: Bolton translates documents on, 58, 62–63
Phillips, Ulrich B., 28
Pike, Zebulon Montgomery: Bolton researches on, 58, 59
Prescott, William: contrasted with Turner, 3

*Reader's Digest,* 100
Republican party: Webb's views on, 86–87
Research: *see* individual entries under Bolton, Turner, and Webb

Schlesinger, Arthur M.: corresponds with Turner, 13–14, 15–16
Science: and history, 31–34
Shannon, Fred: attacks *Great Plains,* 80
Shiwetz, Buck: on Webb, 76
*Southwestern Historical Quarterly,* 59. *See also* Texas State Historical Association *Quarterly*
Spanish borderlands: Bolton's definition, 55, 65–66
Stanford University: hires Bolton, 58

Texas State Historical Association *Quarterly:* publishes Bolton, 57–58. *See also Southwestern Historical Quarterly*
Texas, 53, 58, 75–81, *passim*
Transportation: in the West, 84
Turner, Frederick Jackson: *photo, 2;* papers, 3, 4, 5, 10, 34; difficulty in writing, 3–5, 8, 23–26, 31–32; as teacher, 5, 19–20, 28–30, 33; research associate at Huntington Library, 6–7; attitude toward West, 6–8; typical MS page, 7; definition of West, 8; concepts of historical interpretation, 8–10, 10n, 11–12, 21–22, 24–25; methods of research,